Vincent van Gogh

Library of Congress Control Number: 2018944905
ISBN 978-1-250-16886-3

Our books may be purchased in bulk for promotional, educational, or business use. Please contact your local bookseller or the Macmillan Corporate and Premium Sales Department at (800) 221-7945 ext. 5442 or by email at MacmillanSpecialMarkets@macmillan.com.

First published in France in 2015 by Quelle Histoire, Paris
First U.S. edition, 2019

Text: Patricia Crété
Translation: Catherine Nolan
Illustrations: Bruno Wennagel, Mathieu Ferret, Vittoria Macioci, Sophie D'Hénin, Mélanie Ayusawa

Printed in China by RR Donnelley Asia Printing Solutions Ltd., Dongguan City, Guangdong Province

10 9 8 7 6 5 4 3 2 1

Vincent van Gogh

Roaring Brook Press
New York

Childhood

Vincent van Gogh was a brilliant painter.

He was born in 1853 in the Netherlands, the eldest of six brothers and sisters. He was very close with his brother Theo. Over the years, Vincent wrote Theo more than 650 letters!

Vincent's father was a minister. His uncle was an art dealer, selling artwork all over Europe. He was a big influence on Vincent, who loved to draw.

1853–1869

Apprenticeship

When Vincent was sixteen years old, he became an apprentice to his uncle. He traveled to London and Paris, visiting museums and meeting artists. Vincent was a helpful travel companion. He spoke English, German, and French!

Vincent loved art, but he didn't really want to be an art dealer. What *did* he want to be? He wasn't sure. Vincent decided to become a minister, like his father.

———

1869–1876

Preacher

Vincent took a job as a pastor in a coal-mining town in Belgium. The miners' work was difficult. Explosions at the bottom of the mines could be deadly. Vincent gave his belongings to the miners and began spending time with them.

Vincent spoke out fiercely against the dangerous conditions in the mines. His superiors fired him.

Years later, Vincent would create a painting called *The Potato Eaters* that showed the miners' suffering.

—————

1877–1880

Painter

Vincent needed a new career. He moved to the city of Antwerp, Belgium, and began to study painting. He painted a series of self-portraits—thirty-seven pictures of himself.

Vincent's brother Theo had become an art dealer in Paris. He tried to sell Vincent's paintings but didn't have any luck.

_____

1880–1885

Paris

Vincent joined Theo in Paris. At first, he enjoyed it there. He met other artists. He painted scenes of lively streets and pretty gardens. But after a while, he grew tired of city life.

Vincent moved to the South of France.

———

1886–1888

Arles

Vincent rented part of a house that was painted yellow, where he could live and work.

He took long walks in the countryside, carrying his easel over his shoulder. Whenever he saw a scene that he liked, he would stop, take out his brushes, and begin to paint.

———

1888–1889

Trouble

Vincent's friend, a painter named Paul Gauguin, visited him. They spent their days in the countryside. Often they painted the same scenes but in different styles.

The two friends got along at first, but after a while they began to argue. Their arguments became violent. On December 23, 1888, Vincent cut off part of his own ear during a fight with Paul! It was a sign that Vincent's mental health was failing.

—

1888

Irises

Vincent went to a psychiatric hospital for treatment. While he was there, he created around 150 paintings. One of them was *Irises*, inspired by flowers that grew along a path at the hospital.

Nearly one hundred years later, *Irises* became the most expensive painting in the world.

———

1889–1890

Dr. Gachet

After Vincent left the hospital, a physician named Dr. Gachet took him on as a patient and found him a place to live.

Over the next seventy days, Vincent painted around seventy paintings.

———
1890

Last Days

Vincent went for a walk one morning with his painting supplies. It was a beautiful day. But something went terribly wrong. Vincent returned home with a bullet in his chest!

Dr. Gachet rushed to Vincent's bedside. Vincent told the doctor that he had tried to kill himself. Other people said that Vincent had been shot accidentally by a boy from the village. No one knows for sure what happened. Vincent died on July 29, 1890.

Vincent van Gogh was not very well known or rich in his lifetime. But today, he is famous around the world.

——

1890

1850

1853
Vincent van Gogh is born in the Netherlands.

1857
His brother Theo is born.

1869
Vincent becomes an apprentice to his uncle.

1877
He works as a pastor to coal miners in Belgium.

1880
He studies at an art academy in Belgium.

1885
He paints *The Potato Eaters*, which shows coal miners' suffering.

1886
Vincent joins his brother Theo in Paris.

1888
He paints the *Sunflowers* series, which would become one of his most famous series of paintings.

1889
He enters the Saint-Paul de Mausole psychiatric hospital.

1890
Vincent moves to Auvers-sur-Oise, an area close to Paris.

1890
Vincent dies.

1895

1888
He moves to Arles, in southern France.

1888
Vincent cuts off part of his left ear.

1889
He paints *Irises*.

1890
He paints *Portrait of Dr. Gachet*.

Europe

1 Zundert, the Netherlands

Vincent was born here. His birthplace was demolished, but an art center that bears his name was built on the site.

2 Wasmes, Belgium

Vincent worked here as a pastor to coal miners. He once visited a mine and began to speak against the dangerous conditions.

3 Paris, France

Vincent lived for several years in the district of Montmartre, an area popular with artists. He met many painters, writers, and musicians there.

4 Arles, Southern France

Vincent wanted to create a school of painters in Arles, but he was not able to make the idea work. The Foundation Vincent van Gogh Arles, opened in April 2014, commemorates Vincent's stay in the city.

5 Saint-Rémy-de-Provence, Southern France

Vincent was treated at the Saint-Paul de Mausole psychiatric hospital here. The building was originally a monastery. Today it is a cultural center. Vincent's room has been restored for visitors to see.

6 Auvers-sur-Oise, France

This town is located on the Oise River, near Paris. It's home to the Ravoux Inn, where Vincent died.

People to Know

Theodorus van Gogh
(1857–1891)
Known as Theo, Vincent's little brother was an art dealer who supported his older brother all his life. He gave him money, tried to sell his paintings, and got him medical treatment. Theo lived only one year longer than Vincent and was buried by his side in Auvers-sur-Oise.

Paul Gauguin
(1848–1903)
This painter joined Vincent in Arles, but he left after Vincent cut off his own ear. Paul later went to the Marquesas Islands, where he lived until his death.

Dr. Paul Gachet
(1828–1909)
This doctor, artist, and art collector was based in Auvers-sur-Oise. He had many patients who were artists, including Cézanne, Corot, and Pissarro.

Henri de Toulouse-Lautrec
(1864–1901)
Vincent met this well-known artist in Paris. Henri remained a faithful friend to Vincent and attended his funeral.

....

Vincent created about 900 paintings, but only one was sold while he was alive.

....

Vincent painted *Starry Night*, which would become his most famous work, while he was at the psychiatric hospital. Vincent thought it was a failure.

....

....

Vincent painted a large number of self-portraits, mainly because he didn't have enough money to pay models to pose for him!

Vincent appreciated Japanese art. He had a large collection of Japanese woodblock paintings and prints that inspired him.

Available Now

 Muhammad Ali

 Marie Antoinette

 Neil Armstrong

 Blackbeard

 Buddha

 Coco Chanel

Charlie Chaplin

 Cleopatra

 Marie Curie

 Albert Einstein

 Anne Frank

 Gandhi

Frida Kahlo

 Martin Luther King

 Abraham Lincoln

 Nelson Mandela

 Isaac Newton

 Rosa Parks

 Pocahontas

 Vincent van Gogh

Coming Soon

 Joan of Arc

 John F. Kennedy

 Pablo Picasso

 Princess Diana